by Jeff Dombek

*For my brother, **Doug**, and all the other great P. E. teachers I have known and worked with over the years.*

Special thanks to Keith H., Chip B., and Joe S.

Caveman P.E. Teacher

Text and Illustrations copyright © 2011 by Jeff Dombek
All rights reserved
Printed in the United States of America

Book design and layout: Keith W. Heckert

CORN TASSEL PRESS
Columbia, Maryland

Contents

1. On Strike

"Nothing for me Miss Shirley, I'm on strike," I said as I gazed longingly at the golden-brown grilled cheese sandwiches piled on top of one another in the large stainless steel bin.

"Jimmy Peterson, are you feeling okay?" the friendly kitchen manager asked in disbelief.

"Just fine, Miss Shirley," I replied. The steaming buckets of tomato soup looked inviting, too, but I had to keep moving along. The serving cups of canned peaches never looked more tempting as I glided my tray down the sparkling silver railing. But I had to be strong. We all did. We were on strike. It might sound crazy, but here I was, sitting in the cafeteria with every second grade kid in the school, and *none* of us were eating our lunches. One by one, we all went through the lunch line, politely declining everything we were offered.

Everyone except Amanda Denison, that is. Amanda is the 'goodie-goodie' type who never gets into trouble or does anything wrong - ever! The rest of us, on the other hand, didn't eat a thing. No tomato soup, no grilled cheese, no french fries. Nothing at all. Except maybe our chocolate milk.

The day started out like any other day. We rode the bus, ordered our lunches, did our warm-up work, turned in our homework folders, and prepared for reading groups. Regular stuff. Yet here we were just a little while later in the cafeteria shouting, "We're on strike!" over and over as loud as we could. Banging our fists and slamming our trays on the lunch tables created an unbelievable wall of sound. Some of the kids just couldn't take the noise and began covering their ears. Something had to give.

Suddenly, our attention shifted to a flash of yellow bursting through the cafeteria doors. It was Caveman, our favorite substitute teacher. He stopped quickly, gazing across the room like a towering super-hero covered in animal skins. His clothing must have come from at least ten saber-tooth leopards. Caveman's dark

shoulder-length hair began to sway back and forth like seaweed as he bounded through the noisy room. Marching right up to me with a confused look on his scruffy face, he asked in his own funny way, "What going on here? Why no one eat lunch today?"

"We're on strike. No Field Day, no lunch!" I replied.

He scratched his head in bewilderment, paused, and then walked out of the cafeteria towards the principal's office.

2. Breaking News

Like I said, before all this craziness set in, the day began in the usual (boring) way. The morning announcements came on, beginning with congratulations to all the second graders on the Fire Safety Poster Contest, a yearly event which was held last night at the volunteer firehouse. Caveman had been our substitute art teacher for a whole month, and had helped us make the posters in art class. He taught us how to paint fire by mixing red and yellow paints. Only, I didn't go to the reception because I had painted my hand and arm orange instead of my paper. I never did make a poster.

The announcements continued with the word of the day, followed by the thought of the day, and then finally ended with a long list of kids who were celebrating their birthday. At some point, I lost interest and concentrated on stabbing my pink eraser with my new army pencil.

Then it happened. I heard the voice of Mr. Kim, our principal, thanking everyone for coming into the school building so 'nicely' this morning. I was not prepared for what he said next.

"Boys and girls, I'm very sad to announce that Mrs. Bashko badly sprained her ankle last night at the art show. Therefore, we will have to postpone - I mean *cancel* - Field Day this Friday." The news hit like a door slamming me right in the face.

"Whoooooowwaaaaahhhh?" was all I could groan.

"No Way!"

"No Fair!"

"Nu-uhh!" we all protested.

Miss Myers hushed us. I could tell she was disappointed, too. But she knew she was powerless to help. We all were. Every kid in the class had their face in the full 'frown and pout' position. What a lousy way to start the day.

Even Mrs. Lovelace, my reading teacher, wasn't smiling when she came to pick up Billy, Bruce and me right after morning announcements. On a normal day, she would cheerfully call for the 'Three Musketeers', and the three of us would follow her to a small room called the Reading Station. The rest of the class stayed in their seats and worked with Miss Myers, our second grade teacher. The Reading Station was really just a large closet decorated like an old-fashioned train station on the outside. Inside, however, it was all books and all business. I was so lost in my thoughts of misery and woe with no Field Day, I didn't even notice when Mrs. Lovelace arrived.

"Jimmy, come on." Her voice surprised me as I snapped out of my blank stare and feelings of sadness. "Bruce and Billy are waiting for you," she urged again. I dragged myself from my desk and slouched my way down the hallway with my friends. As we stumbled into the Reading Station, I could not stop thinking about the fact that Field Day - my favorite day of the year - had just been taken away. Just like that, it was gone. It looked completely hopeless until Bruce secretly slipped me this note in reading group:

I then passed it on to Billy. As Mrs. Lovelace walked us back to Miss Myers' room, we secretly discussed the plan. It was up to us to save Field Day. Somehow we would get this message to all second graders, and eventually to the whole school. Maybe then, someone would listen to us kids.

3. Game On

Notes spread everywhere about the cafeteria strike. By lunchtime, every second grader knew what to do. As the line leader and the first person to go through the lunch line, I tried to be polite as I moved my tray along the kitchen railing. Yet, I still needed to set the tone for our important mission. By the time I sat down with my empty tray and looked around, there were nine of us at the table, all with empty trays. Billy, Bruce and I began chanting,

"We're on strike!"

"We're on strike!"

"We're on strike!"

Soon, the whole cafeteria was pounding their trays and shouting along with us. Miss Tyler, our lunch monitor, reported what was happening to Miss Myers. Shortly afterwards, Caveman burst into the cafeteria and then quickly exited to tell our principal, Mr. Kim, about the strike. Principal Kim came rushing into the cafeteria, looking confused as he spoke with Miss Shirley, the kitchen manager.

"What am I going to do with 331 grilled cheese sandwiches?" the bewildered cook asked the principal. "I mean 330," correcting herself, remembering that Amanda Denison actually ate hers.

Mr. Kim quickly turned and headed straight for the microphone on the stage, the one usually used by the lunch monitors. There we sat, about to hear Mr. Kim tell us we were all suspended, or maybe something worse. We gradually grew quiet, like someone was slowly turning down the volume on a television remote controller.

"I know you're all upset about this morning's announcement concerning Field Day. I admire your perseverance and your desire to experience a fun outdoor day. And, I have some good news I think you'll want to hear," he said nervously. Good news? A hush came over the cafeteria. Was this a trick?

"I will meet this afternoon with Mr. Caveman who is teaching our P.E. classes while Mrs. Bashko recovers from her ankle injury," he said. "I can't promise you anything," bargained Mr. Kim, "but I'm hopeful we can work something out, and still have our Field Day after all. For now, Miss Shirley, please have these lunch-buyers come through again. This time, the second chocolate milk is my treat!"

News of what the second grade had done spread

quickly throughout the school. All the students were anticipating the afternoon announcements, hoping for the best. It seemed like the longest afternoon ever. As promised, Mr. Kim met with Mr. Caveman about Field Day.

"Well, Mr. Caveman," he stated, "You have already proven yourself as someone who can come through when the going gets tough. The art show at the firehouse was a great success, thanks in large part to your hard work. I know I'm asking for *another* huge favor here when I ask if you think you can pull things together for Field Day by this Friday. So, what do you say? Can you pull it off?"

Caveman scratched his head and appeared to hesitate as he opened his mouth, and then closed it again. Then he slapped both hands on his knees and declared, "Caveman here to help...will do whatever it takes!" Principal Kim smiled, letting out a long slow sigh of relief. "You are terrific, Mr. Caveman! Don't you worry about volunteers; I'll have my secretary type a sign-up sheet right away for all the kids to take home. There'll be plenty of hands on deck to make for smooth sailing," he said with gratitude.

Mr. Kim made the afternoon announcements himself that day, including the news of Field Day's return to the school events calendar. Everyone in Miss Myers' class danced joyfully when those fantastic words finally came over the intercom: "Thanks to Mr. Caveman, *Field Day is back on again!*"

Miss Myers walked over to me and ruffled my hair.

"Looks like you'll have to practice your potato sack racing after all, Jimmy!" she said proudly.

Billy, Bruce and I felt like we had just won a gold medal. With the help of Caveman, we had saved Field Day!

4. Frisbees and Potato Chips

Following dismissal, Caveman headed for the P.E. office. Settling down in his chair, he began to jot lists and scribble notes on all the things that needed to be done by Thursday afternoon. After about twenty minutes, Caveman looked at his notes and lists and began to panic.

"Impossible... how can I do this? I must be crazy. Caveman in *way* over his thick rock-filled head this time!" Though nervous and stressed, Caveman remained determined to make this the best Field Day ever.

The very next day, Mr. Kim handed Caveman a list of volunteers who would assist on Field Day. Caveman tucked it immediately into a stack of papers on his clipboard. Because it was already Wednesday and Field

Day was only two days away, Caveman skipped eating his lunch and headed straight for the storage closet in the gymnasium to locate and organize the enormous amount of equipment needed to pull off such an event.

"...Potato sacks...*check*...tennis balls...tennis-yep...hockey sticks...oh, there they are...bean bags...*check*...basketballs..." he mumbled softly to himself, checking off the items on the supply list as Caveman continued his search for the rest of the equipment.

"Frisbees...*check*...ring toss...*check*...p-p-potato chips?" he said smiling as he discovered a giant bag of ripple-style barbecue potato chips hiding behind a container of tennis racquets. Since he had skipped lunch and was getting hungry, a snack seemed like a pretty good idea. But not until he located the final items on his list. Jump ropes were the last items to be secured. He needed five for the blacktop games.

"..Jump rope...jump...rope...where jump rope?" he said searching everywhere. He lifted the lid from a plastic tub. "Ahah! Now I found you," he said counting five extra-long red and white jump ropes. "Now, time for snack," he said with a hungry grin.

Caveman set his clipboard down and opened the bag of chips. He didn't notice or remember his half-eaten banana creme donut, the most slippery of all donuts, left over from his snack earlier that morning. It was resting peacefully on a napkin next to a cold cup of coffee, just inside the P.E. closet door where he had laid it earlier that morning. As he smiled and shoved a handful of the bright orange chips into his mouth, he took a small but fateful step forward. Walking toward the closet door opening, his right heel pressed against the squishy donut, sending Caveman reeling backwards like a circus clown. Potato chips flew everywhere like parade confetti.

"Yeooooow!" howled Caveman as his sandals fired off his feet like speeding missiles, soaring high into the air and landing right in a basketball hoop adjacent to the closet door. Fortunately, Caveman landed softly in a basket of badminton birdies, which now dangled from his hair like Christmas tree ornaments.

Just as he pulled himself up from the floor, our class arrived for our afternoon P.E. lesson. Miss Myers didn't

even notice the giant pair of sandals tangled in one of the basketball nets. We waited quietly for a few moments, and then our teacher peered into the gym asking, "Mr. Caveman, are you ready for us?"

"Almost," a voice said faintly from the closet. Caveman emerged barefoot and a little shaken up from his fall in the closet.

"Wah - ha - ha - ha - ha - ha - ha!" the class roared.

Miss Myers gave us 'the look,' and we grew silent immediately.

"Mr. Caveman, are you all right?" she asked with concern. "What's in your hair?"

Caveman reached up and yanked a few badminton birdies from his thick locks of hair. He grinned sheepishly and explained,

"Caveman trip and fall in closet, but okay now."

With a confused look on his face, he kept reaching up until he pulled all six birdies from his hair. Then he reached around his back and found the donut stuck to his bottom. What a mess! Even Amanda Denison was snickering. I was biting my lip extra hard so I wouldn't burst out laughing and end up in time out. It didn't work. I laughed so hard I didn't even wait for Miss Myers to send me to 'the wall'. I just walked over and sat myself down.

5. Green Grass and Blue Skies

The next morning I awoke extra early for school, something I only do once a year. Against all odds, my favorite day of the year - Field Day - had finally arrived. As I was getting dressed, I thought about all of the things that had happened: Mrs. Bashko's ankle injury, Principal Kim's cancellation of Field Day, and our food strike in the cafeteria. Then I peeked out of my bedroom window. The sky was so strikingly blue and clear that I knew this would be a marvelous day indeed, and I soon forgot all about the series of unfortunate events that had occurred earlier in the week.

"Yes!" I rejoiced, "No rain!"

When I arrived in my classroom later that morning, I joined a sea of red shirts since that was our team color for the day. Amanda Denison had a shirt with red flowers and hearts - not exactly what you'd normally wear for an athletic contest. But then again, that's Amanda Denison for you. At least it was a red shirt and not a pink one. We lined up and headed out to the fields through the back door of the school. As my feet touched the thick clumps of grass, I gazed in all directions at an army of volunteers positioned at the various activity stations. My heart was pounding as I looked out upon all the equipment and parents surrounding the school. Hula Hoops, potato sacks, bean bags, basketballs, hockey sticks - all guarded by volunteers smiling and ready for an invasion of noisy and excited kids. I smiled back at them when suddenly a loud whistle shrill snapped me out of my thoughts. It was Caveman, about to start the day's events with a few words.

"Boys and girls, moms and dads, teachers and friends," he began, holding a megaphone up to his face. "Is beautiful day to be outside... Students, please politeness and manners to all volunteers, and do your best! At sound of horn, let Field Day begin!" With that, a smiling Principal Kim let out a blast from an air horn, and all the kids raised their arms and shouted with the joy of a hundred birthday parties!

Our first station was the potato sack race. As I already mentioned, our class wore red, but there was also an orange team and a green team. At the end of the day, scores would be tallied up, and the winning team would be treated to an ice cream party!

"Fwonk!" the air horn sounded, signaling for us to

get to our first station. I was second in line for my team. "Tweet-tweet!" went the whistle, and the race began. The orange team jumped their way to an early lead. My teammate climbed out of the potato sack upon completing her laps, and then came my turn. I hopped as fast as I could down and back. I was out of breath when I handed the next person in line the sack, and I collapsed at the end of our line, huffing and puffing. When the race was all over, we ended up in last - I mean third - place. Orange came in first, and green second.

For our next station, we went to the blacktop games. There were four separate activities on the blacktop: Basketball Hot Shot, Dinosaur Bean Bag Toss, Stegosaurus Shoot, and Hula Hoop and Scoop. I was the first to go for my team at the Stegosaurus Shoot. I picked up the hockey stick and spotted my target - a hole in the belly of a large flat board cut in the shape of a stegosaurus.

"Okay, you get three shots. Fire when ready, son!" said Bruce's dad, who ran the station.

Whack!

"Nice shot Jimmy!"

"Woo-hoo... go Jimmy!"

"Go red team!"

With my teammates cheering me on, I set up for my second and third shots. Whack! Whack!

"Right down the middle!"

"In the hole!"

"Yeah, Jimmeeeeeeeee!"

"Three for three! A perfect score!"

We moved on to our next games. The Basketball Hot Shot and Dinosaur Bean Bag Toss were pretty much what you'd expect. I made most of those shots, too. The Hula Hoop and Scoop, however, was a tricky station. While Hula Hooping, you and a partner tried to play catch with a ball and scoop. Every catch meant a point for your team - as long as your hoop was moving. Unfortunately, that dumb hoop was around my ankles before I could even throw the ball. My partner and I scored a big fat zero in that event. Still, by the end of the blacktop games, our team had managed to climb into second place.

"Fwoooooonnnnnnkkkkk!" blasted Principal Kim with the air horn.

"Freeze pops and water break!" blared Caveman's voice over the megaphone. We ran to get our freeze pops, and cooled off in the shade of the giant oak tree next to the baseball backstop. Next, we went to the water station and began hydrating ourselves for the T-Rex Run, our final event, and by far the most grueling physical test of the whole Field Day. Caveman put a whistle to his lips,

"Tweet!"

Without any directions, all of the second graders of Fullerton Lane Elementary knew where to go. Like a magnet, the far corner of the grassy field drew us all to a line painted in the grass. This is where we all would begin the race, but only the top three runners would earn points for their team. First place meant 25 points for your team, second place earned 10, and third place would add 5 points to your team's final score. We all read the scoreboard during water break. We were behind by 16 points. It was now winner-take-all; only a first place finish in the T-rex Run would help our team. Anything less - goodbye ice cream party.

F.L.E.S. FIELD DAY
SCOREBOARD

Green 497

Red 481

Orange 479

6. Stampede!

The frozen treats had cooled us off for the exhausting run we were about to begin, but it left us all with colored lips and tongues. We looked ridiculous with our cherry, grape and sky blue lips as we prepared for the serious run ahead of us. Following a course of bright orange cones, we would circle around the entire field of grass which surrounded our school. Caveman held the whistle to his lips and gave it a loud blast. With that, the whole second grade was off and stampeding like a herd of red, orange and green buffalo.

Halfway through the course, my heart was pounding and I could feel myself slowing down. I was in fourth place behind my teammate Bruce.

"Go...on...Bruce," I said, gasping between my words, "It's up...to you...now..."

Almost on cue, Bruce took off like a red flash and quickly moved into second place, passing the runner from the green team. Glancing behind him with a worried look, the orange runner in first place could sense Bruce gaining on his heels. With every stride bringing him closer to the leader, Bruce seemed to be going faster and getting stronger.

"Go Bruce, go!" I yelped hoarsely from my distant fourth place position. Remarkably, with about fifty yards to go in the race, Bruce actually took the lead! The whole red team cheered wildly.

Then it happened. With the ice cream party all but locked up for our team, the unthinkable happened. Bruce's baseball cap fell off of his head. What he did next, no one can explain. He stopped. Just *stopped*. Then he started to turn around as if to retrieve his fallen cap, only to suddenly realize what was at stake. However, by the time his feet were moving again, he had lost the lead. Ten seconds later, he had lost the race. The orange team began celebrating their victory, bouncing around like a bunch of overjoyed cheese puffs. *Our* ice cream party was now *theirs*. Unbelievable. Just

unbelievable.

The sad walk back to our classroom was long and quiet. Of course, no one felt worse about losing the ice cream party more than Bruce. Billy and I broke the silence of our long stroll back to class by trying to cheer up Bruce.

"It's okay, Bruce," I said. "You're still the fastest runner in the class by far."

"Yeah," Billy agreed. "If it weren't for you, we'd have no hope of even coming close to winning."

Bruce could only mutter, "What was I thinking?" over and over to himself. I don't think he heard a word we said to him.

Suddenly, Caveman appeared from behind us and put his big hairy arms on our shoulders. "You three make Caveman proud. If not for you crazy boys, this day not happen at all. *Cafeteria strike* - you guys *nuts*! No matter what place you come in, you still champions in my book!"

Bruce finally cracked a smile as Caveman patted us on the back and asked us if we could help collect bean bags and hockey sticks from the blacktop games. Seconds later without warning, Bruce darted off, running as fast as he could away from the school building. Startled, Billy and I looked at each other, not knowing what to do.

Finally, I shouted to him, "Bruce! Bruce! It's gonna be okay, Bruce! Where ya goin', Bruce?"

Bruce took a few more steps, looked down, and then turned around.

"I forgot my hat!" he hollered back.